*The
Dear
Dance
of
Eros*

The Dear Dance of Eros

Mary Mackey

Fjord Press
Seattle
1987

Some of the poems in this volume have previously appeared in:
Split Ends (Berkeley, CA: Ariel Press, 1974) (ed. Mary Mackey)
One Night Stand (Emeryville, CA: Effie's Press, 1976) (ed. Bonnie
  Carpenter)
Skin Deep (Arlington, VA: Gallimaufry Press, 1978) (ed. Mary
  MacArthur)
and the following magazines:
  Yellow Silk: Journal of Erotic Arts (Albany, CA; ed. Lily Pond)
  *Landing Signals; Hard Pressed; Jumpcut; Libera; Anthology of
  Contemporary California Women; The Bright Medusa; Country
  Women; Ms. Magazine.*

Editors: Steve Murray & Tiina Nunnally
Cover design: Art Chantry & Bonnie Smetts
Book design & typography: Fjord Press Typography
Printed by: Edwards Brothers, Inc.

Published and distributed by:
Fjord Press
P.O. Box 16501
Seattle, Washington 98116
(206) 625-9363

Library of Congress Cataloging in Publication Data:

Mackey, Mary.
  The dear dance of Eros.

  1. Love poetry, American. I. Title.
PS3563.A3165D4 1986   811'.54   86-7612
ISBN 0-940242-16-8 (lib. bdg. : alk. paper)
ISBN 0-940242-17-6 (pbk. : alk. paper)

Printed in the United States of America
First edition, February 1987

Contents

The
Dear
Dance
of
Eros

Skin Diver

swimming in the Caribbean
I saw a manta ray
rise from the sand
and ripple the great
wing of her body
through the glass-blue
water

and my breath
caught against the bubble of
my throat
as she moved out
beyond the reef
into the inconceivable black push
of the open sea

I have gone down for her since
my manta
again and again
fished the dark waters
of my night dreams
and the shallow reefs
of my days

I have tracked her
through salt, and sleep

and love
felt her tremble
in the flesh
of a strong man
gone gentle
felt her lift
and fall back again
like the thrust
of the waves

I have imagined
that if I opened my eyes
quickly she would
be there above me
dark circle of flesh
carved out of my sky
primordial as the
first contraction of passion
complete in herself
as a piece of whole cloth

she is my dark lady
this fish
I feel her absence
as parted lovers feel
the phantom pressure
of each other's bodies
I miss her
as I miss the dead
I have loved

I look for her
in the eyes of strangers
I curse the water
that leaves no tracks

I wait for her return
as I wait
for my own youth
to come back to me
swimming in one morning
salt-crusted
on the first heave of the tide.

Turning and Turning in My Arms

turning and turning
in my arms
you become the unmentionable
mystery
the living flesh of love

moving as quickly
as the blades of a fan
blurred into existence
only for an instant
unsubstantial and lovely
you haunt me
like a memory had in advance
out of joint
out of time
and sweetly out of season.

Chamber Music

the touch of your hand
is so sweet
I could tune myself to it
like a tympani

> always
> I have wanted
> one true friend
> but the music
> was wrong
> off key
> a band of gorillas
> scraping along
> flat and untuned
> playing Lawrence Welk
> and John Philip Sousa
> filling up elevators and malls
> but not the human heart

the staccato clutter
of facts in my mind
is only the lumber
of my soul
the crash of warped boards
being thrown into a pile
full of rusty nails, sharp points,

soft pine and splinters
no one could carve
a Stradivarius from it
or even fashion a flute

the truth is
I know nothing
but the music you bring me
I am simple as a child
humble before this miracle
as if I had been deaf
for twenty years
and then one morning
I rose to mute birds
and Bach
suddenly exploded in my brain

always I have wanted
one true friend
but the music
was wrong

now I see
I was like the tree
consuming sunlight
eating oxygen
exuding myself in silence
ring by ring

facts are only
the lumber of my soul
scraps from tacky
Cartesian condos

underneath I am hardwood
black zebra
clean cocobola
ready to turn at your touch

you have lathed me smooth
carved my stops
I have a grace with you
I never knew I possessed
when at last
you raise me to your lips
your breath becomes
my music.

The Invitation

dip down my darling
I am young and bare
I can play your bones
till your teeth rattle reggae

dip down my darling
I can turn your tongue over
and tan your skin into drums
I can play you back
your own jazz
and make
Jamaica

dip down my darling
I can tattoo notes on your fingertips
I can rub a riff
on your lips and hips
I can make you wail and moan

dip down my darling
I can play you, I can sway you
I can virelay you
I can blow you
like a sweet saxophone.

We Made Love Until I Couldn't

remember my name
out on the borders of
morning where everything was snow
white hot like grits
and cream

the smell of your salt was on
my back and there were long
tunnels where buses became beasts
from the Pleistocene I saw
pterodactyl wings sprout
from your fingers felt
the rush of your breath fanning my
neck how naked it all was all those tiny
blond hairs my spine hanging like
a necklace down your chest then
the walls collapsed and the whole room fell
down my throat like a deck of cards

you curled back
my head and held my mouth
open like I was
a rattlesnake
and we began all over
again

god save us I thought this is
madness

but you were man
sweet and not
to be resisted
and my tongue became a song
bird and I wanted to walk
through your body
and come out the other
side in that land
where lovers live in each other
forever
like fish.

Night Comb

oh your hair!
when I smell it
I dream of orchards full
of almond trees
and the slow drift
of cedar smoke

oh your hair!
I feel it rising up over me
like a crest of soft
foam waiting
to break across my breast

it is my land
of dream paths
a trail that winds
through the first jungle
that ever grew
I feel it against my bare skin
and think of pale
golden trees sitting
in dark pools
of heavy, slick leaves
as large as my tongue
of strange, sleek birds

and naked human creatures
discovering love
for the first time

oh your hair!
it lingers in my hands
like the touch of a silk
blanket
it tingles
between my fingers
like a fine spray
I want to dive into it
follow its smooth wake
until I am lost and tangled
the way the ocean is lost and tangled
in the horizon
the way a great forest is lost
and tangled in itself
the way we are tangled and lost
each night
in those great white ropes
of sleeping flesh
that lovers
throw out like fishlines
to snare each other.

Blue July

at two thirty-three
I place the flat of my tongue between your lips
like a wedge
my words
become a school of silver fish
swimming toward you through the molecular
    structure
of your most crystalline dreams
to feed on the simple darkness
at the back of your throat

(at four o seven the air smells of blackberry
    brambles
jonquils and blood
downstairs in a yellow kitchen
a woman is ironing
heavy linen sheets for our bed
water slick with undissolved starch
splashes from the perfect oval
of a brown bowl
over her bare feet)

at that very instant your mouth opens to mine
I taste ambergris and musk
the fan on the ceiling makes a mandala
later, some time after five,
I dream I'm a dolphin
playing in the wake of your breath.

Hibernating at High Elevations

love gathers around us
like an imperfection
in light
like a sheet of plastic
visible only by a long
lateral fold
seaming us together

under the quilt
we are like bears
in ice caves
nose to nose
fur steaming with fall fat
like ants snug
in an underground hive
remembering with nostalgia
plump aphids and summer picnics

hiding from the cold
California rain
two hibernating squirrels
we dream of a simpler life
snowed in at 10,000 feet
the long Canadian winter
muffling us in drifts

buried in each other's arms
under white wolf pelts
no salt jerky
cold hearths
dry beans or boredom here   .

only a single blue flame
climbing up the chimney
straight stalked as an exotic asparagus

you catch it in the palm
of your magically invulnerable hand
and feed it to me

I eat cold fire from your fingers
warm fire from your lips
I am fed
.   and fed again

around us the long winter
turns slowly
as the revolutions of Saturn.

Hike

you carried a compound bow
a box of wax-dipped matches
and a copy of *Stalking the Wild Asparagus*
I carried a micro computer
two hundred floppy disks
and Arthur Naiman's *Introduction to WordStar*

at our first campsite
you trapped, gutted and roasted a beaver
while I wrote a review
of an imaginary critique
of dialectical materialism

at our second campsite
you built a log cabin
with your bare hands
made some pemmican
from cranberries
and carved me a comb

I was wild by then
my permanent had grown out
my leg warmers had raveled
and my batteries were running low

you took me in your arms
and convinced me
that in the spring
you could make me an AC adaptor
from wild mint, honey, and chipmunk teeth

gently you unplugged me
and placed the palms of your hands over
my eyes
when you took them away
I saw again
like a child
the unfluorescent gaudy
spread of the sky
and at the edge of the meadow
three buffalo
parading slowly in a line
shadows scattered over the yellow grass
like rugs
their bodies blue mountains
against the black hills.

Plum

living with you
for a few days
heavy scent of the night
honey suckle at my breast
slow walking
potsherd walls

your favorite apples
were green and hard
Australian apples
that tasted of kangaroo

you ate them with a knife
like your father
and when you were drunk
you wanted me at least

lady flower, you said,
white bloom,
oh you petal arms.

Love and Other Major Disasters

passion is like anthrax
or the bubonic plague
I kiss the open palm of your hand
and think
cicatrice, wound, stigmata
(nothing can cut me away from you
alive)

passion is like the earthquake
that topples the house
piles of plaster
a kettle incongruous on a broken stove
and somewhere the hiss of leaking gas
(you see I would destroy everything
for you)

passion is like the typhoon
that breaks off the palm trees
swamps the island
batters the fish against the beach

passion feeds on disaster
like flies feed on meat
down deep
in the cone of the volcano

in the burning house
the head-on collision
the place where the road is always littered
with fresh glass

(a siren passes by
underneath our window
with five thin bones
you pull down the shade.)

If Love Were a Potato,
I'd Probably Be Idaho

my friend is confused
he doesn't know what to say
I have come down on him
like a swarm of bees
struck with my kiss
like a rattlesnake to the throat
I have put on a fur coat
and imitated a bear
tap-danced on his ceiling
cooked him a six-course
gourmet dinner
complete with escargots

in three weeks
I have made love to him
200 times
given birth to four
of his children
nursed them
fed them cooked carrots
and sent them off to school
now I am ready
for a polite
old age

I remember the touch
of your fingers on my spine
I tell him
your breath
tastes like chocolate cupcakes
I want to tell you
about the Middle Ages
you have snake hips
and muskrat eyes
and pastel shirts
and an earring in your ear
you twist cocktail straws
into kinetic sculptures
you drink gin
and make love
like a slow boat to China
I want to wrap your body
in a pink feather quilt
and sew up your heart
in a bag of light

not so fast
he begs me
let's take our time
he wants the months to be months
and the days days
he's a sensible man
who wants his seconds
to pour by methodically
like sand in a glass

but my love
has no meter
or measure
it comes every seven years
like a convocation
of locusts
it descends
like grace
or god
or pentecost
and I can no more contain it
than I can turn back
the sea from
the land
and it is a gift beyond all blessing
and it is a country of
its own

and I am not
a slow woman
I am a woman
who takes the turns on two wheels
and drives in finger fast
straight for the heart.

What Do You Say When a Man Tells You You Have the Softest Skin

do you say
it's progesterone, progesterone makes it soft?
when he says
you have big brown eyes
do you say
of course
I'm nearsighted?

my body grew in rings
like a tree trunk
at the center I'm always 10
at the center I'm always wearing
pink plastic glasses
braces
wire wrapped around my head
a mouth full of rubber bands
I have buck teeth I can spit through
corrective shoes
pimples
no legs
no butt
no breasts

one day my mother buys me falsies
overnight I grow from 28AA to 36D
I look down and notice I can't see my feet
I feel like a fork-lift
I imagine they are realies

in gym the girls steal my bra
and throw it in the pool
my rubber breasts float away
like humpback whales
I dive for them
over and over
I dive for my breasts
and come up flat

what do you say when a man tells you
you're beautiful?
do you tell him
"I'm still fishing
I'm still fishing for my body."

Don't Put Me in Your Toaster Oven, Honey. I'm Not a Patty Melt Man.

I come to you
holding love in my hands
like ripe plums
this is the fruit
I say
which most resembles
the human heart

you pick up
a chair
and beat me back
as if I were a lady
lion
looking for lunch

no commitment
you say
climbing up on
the table
and upsetting the
sugar bowl
no commitment
you cry
leaping to the mantel

no promises
no future
don't count on me
I won't be there
no better
or worse
gotta keep my guitar greased
and my traveling boots on
hang loose
move fast
stay naked as
a rope

stand back
lay off
give me room to breathe
don't hogtie me woman
with your love
and your tomorrows
with your wedding ring
mind and your two
hundred unfertilized eggs
don't put me in
your honey box
toaster oven
marriage cage
punjab sticks
in the bed

takin' out the garbage
mowin' the lawn
zipping up your
zippers

my daddy
went that way
and he never
came back
thirty-seven years
under other people's sinks
in Twin Falls Idaho
near the mountain
where an old Crow
warrior
ate his enemy's heart
and then went back
home to a crazy wife
who cut it
from his throat
like a bone

and I'll never love a woman
like my daddy did
damn his soul
and I'll never let a woman
swallow me
whole

and I said
honey
I'm a vegetarian
and I'll tell you
something true
I don't eat men
and you don't look like
tofu.

The Yale Professor

I met a man who had been to China
he was a communist, he said,
I talked with Chairman Mao, he said,
I went, he said, to serve the people
Science for the People
Science for Everyone
(he was a professor
at Yale
his research involved implanting electrodes
in the human brain
to control
human emotions
he was a Yale professor
tenured
divorced
with four mistresses
all graduate students
he was a Yale professor
funded by the CIA)

sleep with me, he suggested,
putting his feet up on his desk
I've been to China
sleep with me
serve the man who serves the people.

One Night Stand

You were a four-star fuck
you went on and on
like meditation
or ballet
executing impossible leaps
adopting positions
previously attempted
only by pretzels.

At the end
I had
an urge
to rise up clapping
and cry
"Encore!"

But I had
accidentally
gotten myself
snarled in you
like a fishline.

"Excuse me," I mumbled,
apologetically, trying to disengage,

"I didn't mean
to feel
any tenderness.
You see
I suffer from the delusion
that making love
makes love.
I hold the insane
conviction
that people
should be more than bags
for each other's phantoms.
I imagined
that if I reached
into you
I could pull out
the eagle
that is beating itself
to death
against your ribs,
and stroke it
back to sleep."

"Excuse me, please.
I am undergoing
therapy
to cure me of
the habit of caring

and someday I hope
to be
as sane and cold
as any normal
American."

"After all
in my lucid interludes
I know
I'm only one
of the hundreds
who came down the road
and pulled in briefly
at your
one night stand."

The Loves We Walk Away From

just for a moment
you run your hands over my shoulders
and down my back
while I hurry toward my door
pretending not to notice

goodnight
goodnight
it's the loves we walk away from
that we remember the longest
the life we imagine
that we live out in the end

that night I dream
of you and me
standing in the garden
that your old girlfriend planted
vines climbing up to our hips
paths padded with yarrow and comfrey
fat bees hanging heavy in the air
on rafts of yellow pollen

we speak carefully in low voices
about a certain place
where we will meet the next day:

two cypress trees
a white house
a patch of blue lupine
the wild ducks will be there too
you say
and once again you run your hands over me
this time I feel a whole future
explode between us
clean and empty as a tin dipper

but when I wake
I know that the place isn't there
that the address you gave me
is for a street that never existed
in a city
neither of us can name.

Very Early in Marriages

I wake each morning
to the sound of frogs
penny whistles
rubber bands
two cups clinked together

I am naked on a cot
naked in the tropical heat
the canvas sticks to my back
like a shell
turtle naked

above me the bats
have settled into silence
their sonic squeaks are muffled
drowned in the first frogs
sleeping female bats
nurse their young
bags of fur hanging over my cot
like a rack of wigs

beside me
my husband is sleeping
purple in the early morning light

he sleeps so quietly that
I am afraid
afraid he has stopped breathing
died in the night
I lean over him
open-mouthed to catch his breath

oh it is very early in marriages
5 or 6 o'clock
when we first wake up and see
the bodies of the dead.

Juliet

I was a green girl
fourteen and fresh
my breasts curled
so tight in my chest
that they ached
time pulled through
my body like sap
and I thought love
grew everywhere
like milkweed

Romeo was a human
swagger
we drove over the state
line near the end
of spring
and were married by
a judge in striped
pajamas
who loaned us a
cigar band
for a ring

I said
look how the dogwood is
in bloom
like the lips of small children
in the naked woods
and Romeo said
let's stop
for a cheeseburger

I said
when I see the river
I imagine a mouth
at the end
that could swallow us
both

I said
this is the beginning
of a great adventure
I said
I have escaped
into love
and I'll never be
unhappy again

but there was wax
to take off the kitchen floor
and diapers to wash
and Romeo snored

and I found that love
grows around the heart
like the bark on a
tree
and we had three
children
and nobody died
and you can wait forever
for the balcony scene.

The Botanical Garden

under a cactus in the botanical garden
a green tin sign: *Mammilia pulchra*
(the beautiful breast)

we haven't made love for six months
Lisa said
Ben and me there's a cold war on
and the baby keeps crying every time
we get in bed and even if I shut her
in the next room I can feel her
crying go through me like electricity
it makes the hairs on my arms stand on end
my body go numb
it stings my tongue and I taste copper pennies
instead of Ben's mouth

my baby crying if I could only
get some rest then maybe Ben and I could
but my baby
I can't
leave
nursing she needs
you see these stains on my blouse?
my breasts
even when she cries two rooms away
it comes down

milk like an ocean
you can drown in it
and look at these bougainvillea
the buds like thumbs or nipples
and there I go again
my baby I take her everywhere
her mouth nursing out even my dreams
and Ben says we should get away together
to Mendocino because I never get
a full night's sleep

strings on my spine a puppet
jerked stark awake
sitting on the edge of the bed listening
is she hungry?
does she need me?
feeling my breasts at night
swell towards her

this sage smells good
like fried chicken and from this hill
you can see the City and I haven't been
out of the house in the longest time
and those goldfish remind me of my
psychiatrist he has a whole tank full
and a maid to clean the water
and he says I should give her the bottle
and Ben says it's unnatural sitting up
at night like that all the time to listen
I count her breaths

and even now you see these stains on my blouse
she is crying somewhere

mammilia pulchra
all those spines
a painful plant
with a ring of dry nipples
where the flowers should be.

Separate Beds

in the livingroom
you have made
a nest of dry leaves
and bones
like a wolf
you have piled
fresh killed things
around you
rabbit skins
and dead dreams
and cushions stuffed
with my hair

in New York
your body
curled into mine
like black paper
stuck to me
like a silhouette
your bones
were like a cheese grater
and your eyes
were hot yellow stones

in New York
when we were young
and poor
and hungry
and sick
we held each other

now two doors
cut our love
in half
the taxidermist has
stuffed our lives
we keep them
in separate boxes

back in our bed
I sleep with pennies
on my eyes
and even the cat
finds my body
too cold to touch.

Let Not to the Marriage
of True Minds

when you won't
make love to me
I become sullen
I wear dirty flannel
sweatshirts to bed
and sleep in my socks
I slam cold beans
down on the table
and never take out
the trash

the kitchen becomes
a mirror of our lives
grease gathers in the
sink
and there are funny stringy
things in plastic cups
in the refrigerator

the ice in the freezer
is too thick to cut with a
cleaver
we stick like ants
to the linoleum floor

dirty laundry piles up
in the corner
and the dishcloth would
make my mother sick

I withhold water from the plants
and watch the ferns die
with glee
the cat's dish is a national
disgrace
there are worms in the flour
I can outlast you

I know this is a perverse
seduction
and I say you will have to take me
as I am
and love me
my fat thighs
my stringy hair
my sweet cold feet
on your belly.

Rubbing Two Sticks Together

cold nights
cold nights
this bed is too crowded
to be so empty
so lonely
we're sleeping alone together again tonight

you lie on me
arms, legs
flung on me
I am trapped in a cage
of fallen trees
flesh jackstraws
a jumble of bones
your fingers close over my face
like living bars
you have been cut down
and tonight I am pinned
under your trunk
I can feel the termites at work
beneath your skin
there are splinters
on the sheets

my dreams are a dark forest
oak and maple, hickory and pine,
catalpa, elder, buckeye tree,
slippery elm, sassafras
I smell the bark
the wet leaves beneath our mattress
I lie, and look, and watch the limbs
sifting the light above my head
filtering our bedroom walls
stem, twig, branch, trunk
I lie uprooted beside you
my feet are exposed
tendril toes sucking at air
I am uprooted
I am brushwood
drying in this bed
you are dead
dead beside me
dead wood

we are both clear-cut
fallen, felled
nothing lives in us now
the birds are dead
the deer have gone
only the bears sleep somewhere
perhaps
beneath us

we are clear-cut
stumps
tinder
we lie
dry
rubbing together
waiting for our match.

Rain Dance

streets like dry
tongues running down to the
river
mud, shallow
water, a comb of stones
the dust of dead
ladies' clubs
a hesitation
waltz

your body fits
mine like a plug fits a
socket
heat lightning
the sky curled like a pan
of cracked mud
sheets sticking adhesive
tape
sweaty and sucking
fans and flies and flesh
on the altar
four posts and sacrifice
perfect without blemish
our rain
dance our ritual
the Hopi

praying
in Kachina masks
the tempo of dolls pounding
the desert dry
mesas dancing
two thousand feet into
a sunset that crackles like
cellophane

chanting
chanting

give us rain
weep on us
the corn is dry in its
shucks
we are thirsty our land
rises up and blows
away on the wind
our fields are black
there is no water
bracken and scum
and alkali salt
our children are drying
like strips of deer meat

above the city the clouds
are seeded
thunderheads gather at the foot
of our bed

the dancers hold
snakes in their mouths dry
scales that curl
like the tendrils of bean plants
parched in the sun
your lips against mine
leaves without stems
rhythm
rhythm
everything is
rhythm the dance
and the chanting begging
for water until the
ground itself
heaves up and crashes
against the horizon tidal
waves of dust and
supplication

the sand painting holds
the world at its center together
we beat down the rain
from the sky.

Into Tenderness

tenderness

tenderness
it is turning

lust is turning
into
into
into
tenderness

my hand
barely scraping
the hairs on
your chest
like the wind
passing through
the grass
rippling
sun reflecting
in each blade
a separate sun
bending and breathing
my hand

the breath
of you passing
under me
painting you
with heat
with the heat
of my palm
painting you
with heat
brushing on
energy
stroke by
stroke passing
across you
hair by
hair

bend
bow
I sculpt
you beneath
my hands
I recreate you
as the blind
recreate vision
with my fingers
I listen to
your breath

as the deaf
listen to the
vibrations of
a symphony

I see you
newly made
as if I had
just turned you
on a potter's wheel
or pounded you
from brass
as if I
had just
borne you
slick and down
soft
with curled hands
wet and blind
from between my
legs

you are new
to me
each time
I touch
you

tenderness
tenderness

you are new
to me
each time
I touch
you

fragile as a stem.

Each Day Has Its Poem

each day has its poem
the morning rain drowning the garden
the sick child hugging the cat
burned bacon and toast and grease in the skillet
sewing the curtains so we can make love
right down there on the livingroom rug
without Steve our eight-year-old neighbor
selling tickets to all his friends

each day has its poem
hoeing and raking and doing our taxes
as exotic as Martians
with our secret hates and broken dishes
you throwing the stew
me waiting mean and sneaky
like a black widow spider
to give your old shoes to the Goodwill

our morning kisses
unwashed mouth perverts
defying Ipana ads
licking like cats at each other's breath

love before coffee
coming hungry and groggy
into the couplet of another day.

Don't Tell Me the Sea Is a Woman

don't tell me
the sea is a woman
Neptune with his salad fork
the Greeks knew better

the old man is cunning
he poses as water
while his waves feel up
the beach

brain lobes of coral
octopus arms
sperm whales schooling
past the wrecks
of dead lady ships
who went down politely

ancient seducer
you draw me down
until I forget breath
the desire of breathing

I spread my legs
and you enter me
salty and smelling of fish

my naked body
dissolves in the diving.
I can taste you
to the backs of my eyes.

Soft Soap

you pull me into the bathtub
with you
the lukewarm water
laps over my legs
    (dirt under your nails
    you work harder than I do)
my hair sticks to my lips
there is a moth
flying into the light
over the sink
the water is gray
and hard
and someone has used up
all the soap
and your eyes
are made out of blue
tile ceramic in your
face and your desire
floats to the surface
white, clean, and naked
and if this is not love
my dear
it is an acceptable
imitation.

Love Junkie

sex isolates us
we lie in bed all day
shooting the smack
of warm bodies
nakedness
building a thing that has no place
for other people
that digs no tunnels
that does no work

shoot me up again on love
let me nod out

I dream dreams
see visions of naked faces
blind bare faces
hurt past all hatred
children in a burning village
covered with burning plastic
the burning bamboo roof cracks
like a burning Christmas tree
burning fronds fall
like fourth of July snakes
burned children run back and forth
barefoot torches
with burnt-out eyes

shoot me up again on love
shoot me up on love
shoot me up on love
let me nod out

I see a tunnel
a long dark tunnel
I close my eyes
but it stays
like a scratch on my cornea
a long hollow scratch
tunnel full of bodies
rats, water, gas
in front of a dead child
a bowl of rice has been turned
upside down
outside a GI is throwing canisters
lobbing them one by one
into the mouth of the tunnel
his gas mask makes him look
like a giant wasp
killing the dead
over and over
just to make sure

shoot me up on love again
close my eyes
touch my breasts
tell me I'm not to blame
make me warm

70

love me
lay me
fuck me
erase me
shoot me up on love again

shoot me
please.

Third Time Under

time keeps slipping away
down river
down river

maybe I'm drowning again
going down
going under

maybe I never was a swimmer
after all

there was a time when I thought
I could walk on the water

now
I put my body in cold channels
strike out
for just the hope
of a shore.

Love Song

September ago I
came into the white
into the white
the light place
with empty halls
into the rooms where the nurses wear white
where the beds are white
and much too clean

    well made beds without a stain
    sheets no lovers ever rolled on
    hemmed, starched, rigid as death
    tight as the heads of calfskin drums

they let me lie
wrapped in those sheets
alone
wrapped in a cloth cocoon

    (people came in and talked
    they said:
    it won't take long
    it's very simple
    you'll never know

never remember tomorrow
that you were . . .
that you were . . .)

they straddled my feet
I felt the metal
felt the stirrups hit my soles
felt my womb jump in terror
shrink from the lights
the cold green lights
that ring of faces
smiling, saying:

> *open up love*
> *open your legs*
> *this is a love song*
> *to knives and metal*
> *gas, needles, orgasms of pain*
> *this is a love song*
> *let us in*
> *this is a love song*
> *open your legs*

I saw them surround me
masked like a chorus
they pried me apart
and came all at once
scraping, cutting, cleaning me

I'm very clean now
ever so clean
cleaner than sheets
cleaner than metal
empty and clean
empty and clean
empty and clean

cleaner than knives.

The Museum of Unnatural History

in bed
you cover me with your sweat
as if it were a blanket

and my hands tremble
and become huge fans
ribbed and ceaseless
they beat out
the last measures
of our love

     your body is like
     a forest in a museum
     heavy with plaster trees
     and fake grass

and me at the center
imitating
a bird.

A Poem for All Prisoners

I have been a teacher of tenderness
a wet nurse to pain
I have cut keys to lost locks
entered rooms without doors
walked through walls thick as death
thrown open the prisons of the heart
and seen the skeletons embrace

but like a broken arm
the mind finally molds itself
to the cast that surrounds it
and after a while
every prisoner becomes
his own guard

I have watched you patrol
your own periphery
confiscate contraband emotions

I have beaten myself against you
breathless
like a moth against a light

but there are no visiting days

the skin search goes on
I suspect you of harboring concealed passions
I have felt you tremble
shake yourself down
shoot yourself trying to escape.

Coda

you said I was the apple
and you were the stem

that was when I was connected
to time
by your body

now my clothes aren't my clothes
and my house isn't my house
I look in the mirror and see
some stranger with pale blue skin
holding her head in her hands

I do not like to see my bed
it reminds me of the nights
black curtains at the window
your dreams marching through mine
like Caesar's legions

I am putting an ad in the paper
asking for another love at discount rates
striking a hard bargain like a match head
hot and short

the future feels
like something
I could break my
nails on.

The Shadow Puppets

we were not bent upon destruction
but curved to silence

we thought we were like the knife blade
bowed beneath the water
we thought that nothing moved
but the image
we thought that the thing behind the image
stayed frozen forever in the instant
like a single frame of film
we thought we were like people in a painting
forever beginning to sink
and never sinking
we thought we were petrified in amber
like a pair of bees
caught in a million-year-old flight
to some extinct flower

we were not bent upon destruction
we thought we never moved

but destruction like a long shadow
with many hands at evening
danced along the road before us
the shadow puppets
the idiot couples
who ate each other
while we stood still.

Snow

Mama, Mama, come get me quick.
This here cocaine's 'bout to make me sick.
                              — Folk song

you joined the expedition
to the pole
pulled out on your sled
leaving me behind

you disappeared
over the rim
of the great white horizon
of the world
on iced runners
like a spot of ink
falling off the page

the first blizzard
numbed your nose
the second your gums
the third your throat, your lungs,
your hands, your heart
finally your soul crystallized like a geode

and you were drifted in
for a long winter
and your days were all darkness
and your nights anaesthetic
cold and deep

you said you felt no pain
you said you had never done anything
wrong
you said you were always happy
high on the ice
at the top of the world

but you don't walk the same
and you don't talk the same
and your body is as blue as a jazz note
and when you open an envelope
your hands shake
and your words stumble out of your mouth
like crippled birds

and as for love, dear,
I think you fed it
to your dogs.

Finished

nothing is like anything today
the avocado plants droop in the sun
the pumpkins ripen in my garden
they are not moons or globes or children's
     mouths
or signatures or seasons
the dry grass is not a catastrophe of gold
broken by the wind
it is not your beard or hair
or the brush of your fingers along my spine
fine and soft as so many stems

the air rises in blue columns
lifting birds and thistle down and spasms of dust
cleaning love out of the corners of things
sanding me down to the grain.

Sexual War

we have boned each other
like chicken breasts

every year
a necklace of scars

like orb spiders
we clutch the threads
of our webs

(I feel you move
feel you tremble
you are wrapped in silk
tangled in me
like a butterfly.)

After Long Silence

death comes quickly
like a bird wing
across the mouth

three thousand miles away
you hang up the phone
get into your truck
and drive it off a cliff

I hear a silence
that spreads all the way back
across a continent

for years I wonder
what I might have done
to save you

how could anyone who could combine
pink and purple in such perfect balance
catching the exact moment
when the sun moves behind the clouds
how could anyone who could write
that the rain falls in spring
like a black bull leaping a fence
how could anyone who could do these things

fall so awkwardly through space
breaking himself
like some kind of dime-store doll?

it is a disgrace
your end
it has the flavor of a redwood forest
cut down to the stumps
litter on a beach
oil on water
and the taste of good things wasted

the receiver replaced
the long long silence
the static on the line.

The Single Life

you will have to give
back the penny candy
you took as a child
the blue gumballs
and sweaty sugar hearts
the corsages
and rings
and dinners for two

you will have to live
where the flesh is
sweetest
alone and single
and close to the bone

the sun will claw
at you each morning
like a hungry cat
you will have to turn
it back
you will have to embrace
yourself like a lover
in the sheet tent
you pitched last night

eight grains of dust
will lie on the table
there will be a water
ring
the wastebaskets will fill
slowly like limestone pools

your body will become
your body
and your body
alone.

Skin Deep

all day I have labored
in front of my mirror
like a fisherman
trying to haul in a face
snagging an eyebrow
a bit of lash
half a lip swimming past
like a red simper

my mouth is washed back to me
like an old bottle
crusted with barnacles
full of ransom notes
and love letters
and the scum of ancient wines

gills and scales
hair like bleached kelp
waterlogged passions
the slow sinking
the salt in my throat
the years swimming by
one by one
like white-bellied sharks.

Clearing the Land

take a snake
to your bed dear
gray blue
flat-headed thing
so grateful
to curl between
your breasts
animal gratitude
is what we all want
your lips are
stained with the
wine
and there is a red
tinge to your teeth

up on the mountain
the rest of us are
dancing
with grape leaves
in our hair
one woman has gone mad
she lies on the ground
her white wool robe
pulled over her face
keening in the spring

in her hands
there is something
torn in half

she chants that
no one loves her
and that someone
will have to pay

we put her out
like a fire
this is no maidens' ring
we are all veterans
of some hunt or other
we are decorated with
our scars
by nightfall
we will have cleared this land
of everything alive
and begun to feast
upon each other.

Desire

in my dreams
I hold my lovers
next to me all at once
and ask them

what was it I desired?

my hands are full
of their heads
like bunches of cut roses
blond hair, brown hair, red, black,
their eyes are pools of bewilderment
staring up at me
from the bouquet

what was it I desired?
I ask again

was it your bodies?
did I hope by draping
your flesh over me
I could escape
boredom
loneliness
gray hairs shooting
towards me

from the future
like thin arrows?
did I think I could escape,
by taking your breath
into my mouth,
did I think I could escape
the responsibility
of breathing?

what did I desire in you?

sex?
knowledge?
power?
love?

did I expect the clouds to
crack
and blue moths to fly out of the stars?
did I expect a voice
to call to me
saying
"Here at last is the answer."

what
I yell at them
shaking my lovers
what did I desire in you?

their ears fall off like petals
they shed their faces
in a pile at my feet
their bewildered eyes
pucker and close
centers of fallen flowers

the last face
floats down
circling in the darkness

what did I desire in you? I whisper

the stems of their bodies
dry in my hands.

Diet

I grew so thin
and lean
like a shoelace
I had no substance
my hands were bamboo
curtains of bones
I walked through small
spaces
felt my voice
snuff out
at the wick

under my skin
I could see my
heart keeping
time
I could be read
through
I was trans-
parent
I refused all
nourishment
I held my breath

the only sound
I made
was the space
between my words

my goal was to
shed these last few
ounces of living
my goal was to
whittle my flesh
down to the core
cross-hatch my bones
and become pure

hunger.

For the Duration

To Jeffrey Scott Johnson of Tyler, Texas
in celebration of fourteen years of friendship

1.

four marriages between
the two of us
and never to each other
fourteen years of you
cross-hatched through
my life
sleeping with you in Cambridge
before my first wedding night
in a half slum flat
where the heat pipes played *La Traviata*
and the bed was held together
with baling wire
outside the snow
falling in benediction
and I dreamed that night
that you were a pure river
of light
running into me
into my delta self

where the sorghum grew thick
and the cane was sweet
and your breath beside me
was the humming of a single bee
caught in a yellow-throated
honeysuckle vine

and you said you loved
the top of my head
and you touched it constantly
blessing and baptizing
talking in your Holy Roller voice
straight from East Texas
saying you would
be the worst best man
who ever lived
saying you would put
peanut butter in my ring
and steal me from Rob
like Black Jack Davey
on your gypsy appaloosa
in your Sam Houston boots
and your Harvard tie
but I went to the altar
like a paschal lamb
or stewing hen
and you went to Africa to forget me
and I went to Costa Rica to forget you
and that was supposed to be the
end of it.

2.

you were my metronome
my measurer of time
I lost you
I found you
I found you
I lost you
you were as periodic as light
particle and wave
who can span
fourteen years
and find all the rhythms
and beats?
secret letters
and months of indifference
times when I dreamed of you
every night
and times when I forgot
your name

you grew handsome
and a moustache
and wrinkles by your eyes
and I saw my own age first
in the gray of your hair

I had loved a white-lipped boy
Texas drawl
shaky as a pan of dry beans
I had never imagined
he would become a man
who could have guessed
the tree from the seed
or dreamed away the chrysalis?
ten times the lover
you were at twenty
your body and mind
joined at last
keystoned into a single arch
you bear the weight of yourself
differently now
you are one of the solid centers
this planet turns on.

3.

yesterday you came
back to me again
floated in my hot tub
in the house I own
the grown-up house
with the roses in front
and the peeling trim
my eyes looked like holes
in a wool blanket
I hadn't eaten for three days
there was dust on the toast
in the kitchen
and pieces of me on the floor
you put me back together quickly
like a jigsaw puzzle
knowing all the old parts
the slant and fit of me
only you could have
found my borders and corners
so quickly

you said I would survive
you fed me shrimp
you said I had grown to be
a fine woman
you called me by my oldest name
and blessed my hair and head

you put on your tan suitcoat
and glasses
and went out to buy flour tortillas
for your wife
you asked me how I could have married
someone I had only known
three years
your eyes shook like spots
of water on a skillet
the East Texas was still
in your voice
and you spoke of an amazing grace
you had given your body
to be burned you said
and not found love
your family was dead
and scattered
we remembered your father together
playing his steel-stringed guitar
cornbread in his buttermilk
telling us all we were God's precious
diamonds in the rough
and I helped you for a moment
dream back your own past
as if I too were the librarian
of your life

you said you had to leave
but that you would come again
and leave
and come
and come
and leave
here and not here
sweet Mary
you said
and I will be with you always
yes
and not always
for the duration.

The Japanese Garden
at Oahu Airport

the curve of a carp
the comma of a plane
the lilies blow in
holding patterns
two Japanese women
under the willows pose
for the pentax

brown necks
blue orchids
behind them the planes
leave one by one
like metal husks

the women too
give their bodies
to the air
bend and blow
the locust pods
move like fingers
and all seeds
ride the wind

at the bottom of the pool
the mud is deep
and cool
fish touch fish
touch water
scale and skin
the seed falls
and roots
and sprouts
and nothing
flies forever.

The Woman in the Moon

my great-grandmother
married at sixteen
a blue-eyed Irish woodworker
who promised to build her
a life out of apple wood
and cherry
instead he gave her
thirteen children
drank up the rent
and died of blood poisoning
while building a carriage
shaped like a shoe

for forty years
she lived alone
dressed in black
like a retired witch
in a house full of chests
and chairs and wood clocks
waiting for him
to come home again

when she was eighty
and I was four
we met
her skin was so thin

by then that you could
see her veins like grain
she kept her teeth
in a glass of water
and her heart in a rosewood
box by the door

there is a woman
in the moon
my great-grandmother told me
who carries a bundle of sticks
on her back

each month she swells
each month she declines
like many women
she has married a burden
and must bear it forever
across the sky

life bends us, she told me
my own life was scrapwood
my own life was sorrow
as thick as a board

tell all your daughters
to build something better
burn kindling
not carry
keep one eye on the sky.

Bag Lady

I knew a long time ago
that you were going down
I dreamed of lifeboats
and water in the mouth
the first time I saw you

in the opening scene
you are sitting in front of your mirror
looking at the watermarks on the glass
wedding bows all broken
seven years without a birth
you can see at a glance
that the bad times are beginning

> *how dry my skin is*
> *there are liver spots on my face*
> *my great great great grandmother*
> *was burned for a witch*
> *I am feeding the cat fresh cream*
> *and this act I know*
> *will testify against me*

in the next scene you are taking a needle
out of a drawer
but you can no longer see the eye

the threads of your life
have become the filaments of a phantom
behind you the children
are fighting with knives

lint lies in the corners
the bathtub is yellow
I do not move the plants
when I dust them
to tell the truth
I no longer dust
this act I know
will testify against me

in the third scene
you are looking at the side of the bed
where your husband once slept
you are looking at your bankbook
and your children's empty shoes

I'm a widow lady and I live alone
at night I put on the victrola
and play New Orleans jazz
ten years ago
the car swerved into a bread truck
and I was crippled
but I go on dancing just the same

111

I'm a widow lady who wears red
instead of black
this act I know
will testify against me

when you were young
there were no roads
or trucks
only wagons and mud paths
lacing the countryside
mules and windmills
and the clean white waste
of winter snow

now in the last scene
out on Sycamore Street
you mumble to the traffic
an ill-natured old crone
with paper bags full of trash
dragging a roll of asphalt roofing behind you
like a queen's train
and cursing a man dead
these twenty years

oh you had affairs damn you
I knew you did
but I kept my mouth shut
because of the children

may they rot in hell
for never calling
a mother, what's a mother?
a bag stuffed with junk
and fifteen cents for a bottle
I spent my whole life picking up
after other people
and then you had to go and die
damn your eyes
heart attack
I knew you had affairs
when we were first married you called me
your darling baby girl
now I got to catch the number 17 bus
Sam Sam why don't you love me like
you used to
Tommy, Alice, Andy look both
ways before you cross
the ashes to ashes and
dust to I just can
't take it any mo
re   these words
you all   have testified
against me.

In Indiana

in Indiana
the corn comes up sharp
green
like shards of glass
broken glass
broken fields

this spring the whole country is
splintered

my sister walks beside me
grow up strong I tell her
lift weights
push up
have strong arms
strong legs
hands that can crush things

don't be like me
another weak woman
fingers like lace
a paper doll

my sister does not hear me
already she is dancing
barefoot in the corn
her feet turn the earth
her body is straight
hard as a cob
her breasts are small
unripe kernels
her feet turn the earth
my sister is dancing
her feet turn the earth
like the blades of a plow.

Wild Woman

sometimes I imagine I am a frontier woman
lost from my wagon train
wandering
starving
sucking the sweet tips of wild chives
grubbing under the leaves
for beechnuts and acorns
for puff balls gone soft as flesh
stuffed with yellow powder

the snow melts on my tongue
I forget my drawing room
my china cupboard
my ten quilts pieced by hand

at the first thaw
foxes crawl out
leaving warm leaves
old fur
the smell of rotting wood

pulling my hair
I make a snare to catch meat
the wild geese returning
snarl in my net

I coat my skin with their fat
forget my fine complexion
my long white gloves
I am oiled leather now
I shine in the sun
my hair grows long on my head
and under my arms
I spend the night counting the stars
and remembering the husband and children
who, thinking I am dead,
have put up a stone marker

by now
no doubt
I've been carved and dated

they bleed away like ghosts
manless
childless
for the first time
I am not afraid

my feet grow hard as bloodstone
my petticoat falls off
I am naked and tattered
I chew a willow rod to a point
and spear my first trout
I twist my wedding ring into a hook
I survive

at night sometimes I think
I have become the woods
my arms are trees
my fingers twigs
my feet roots
my body disappears like a bad dream

the pools reflect a wild woman
her breath smells of comfrey

I forget the name he gave me
and invent my own.

Betony

by the time
we came across the gap
through the Cumberlands
it was late spring
and I was driving the wagon alone
my husband was buried
under a buckeye tree
five days back
two of the children
had milk fever
and the third lay
sick at my breast

it was a violent
blue-green Kentucky spring
mushrooms raised their humps
over every log
and the waters were roiled
with strange fish

the first year we ate
acorns and nearly starved

you need a husband
the neighbors said

the second year
the cabin burned
and I covered my children
with leaves
and nested down with them
like a squirrel

you can't live without a man
my neighbors told me

the third year
we ate our own corn
at our own table
the forest around us was blessed
we killed nothing
the earth opened up to our seeds
the sun and the rain
came in perfect order
and the squashes in the garden
swelled like pregnant women

I took coltsfoot and barberry
and conceived a fourth child
she was born with a tiny ring
of blood around her wrist
and her eyes were as soft
as new bark
when she walked
wildflowers grew in her footprints

her bones were fine and hollow
she flew over her sisters
like a jackdaw

I called her Betony
and the neighbors said
I was mad

she will grow sweet to the taste
I told them
she will cure all wounds
she will be Betony
the spiked plant
the wood mint
the woman alone
who sanctifies.

The Music Lesson

I loved Mademoiselle
she had long strong
fingers and wore
twenty rings
black lace mitts
on her hands
she had studied
with Debussy
her touch was as sure
as a surgeon's
she kept me at that
great polished piano
in the back parlor
day after day
pounding out the time
against the back of my
head with the heel of
her palm

outside I could smell
the tar on the streets
the apple butter cooking
in a neighbor's kitchen
music must be perfect
Mademoiselle told me
or not at all

her eyes were tiny and dark
and her dress smelled
of lavender and musk
she would take
only the best
when I missed a
note or hurried
the tempo
she would rap me
across the knuckles
with her cane
until tears came
to my eyes
leave the mistakes
to the sloppy girls
with no talent
cherie, she would
say offering me
her handkerchief
afterwards

every day
for one hour
she made me be
perfect
flawless
without a single
hesitation

she taught me that music
was like a breath
breathed for an instant
through me
you are an artist she told me
throwing up the lid of
the piano with a bang
now play your heart
out
later she would feed me
peppermint drops
and tell me of Paris
a room, a piano
and a view of the Seine
she would say
what more could a woman
want?

when I got married
I stopped my lessons
I was afraid to see Mademoiselle
so I never sent
word
three years later
we met on State Street
she had some other girl
with her
a little cheese-faced thing
with a sheaf of music
in her eyes

Mademoiselle looked
at the baby in my
arms and offered it
a peppermint drop
then she bent close
and I could smell the
lavender and musk again
Paris, she said,
you could have studied
in Paris
you had talent
you know
I hid my hands
under the baby
Mademoiselle leaned over
and kissed me on
the cheek
I forgive you, cherie
she said
but the music
la musique
ne pardonne pas.

Arabesque

Five poems for women without children

First Position

don't make so much
noise dear
the nurses say to the woman
three days in labor
white scum on her lips

outside the streets are hot
and flat and infinite
and time is only marked
by the dilation of pain

you're acting like a little girl
the doctor tells her
you don't hurt
hips like a cow
you were born to bear

his own stomach
is pegged across his thighs
like a well-tanned skin
he catches the little bloody
head in his hands

love this
he tells her
even the bones
were made from your teeth.

Second Position

mix honey and semen
in a golden cup

place blood in a cross
on your lips

take off your skirt
and run naked
through the new corn

eat liver and brown bread
let your womb be opened
with a knife

greet your husband with a smile
wear a new negligée

take your temperature
every day

put crushed chili peppers
between your legs

copulate with a snake
confess your sins

cover your body with pitch

drink water from a hollow stump

eat the clay from a newly dug grave

there are children under your skin
you are holding them back
we have come to collect
a tax on your life

you owe us sons

you say you are trying
but we do not believe you
we are waiting here under your bed
for a birth
and a body
and the smell of fresh blood.

Pas de Deux

I step across the threshold
this is such a small
movement it is hardly
noticed

my mother hands me
a blue china cup
half full of milk
the ice is breaking up
on the river
she tells me
the floes catch in her dark
hair
and her hands unfold
like flowers

did you want to be a grandmother?
I ask her
she gives me both her hands
in a single bouquet
and says

let me be the mother
of the mother
of the dance.

Ballerinas

the nuns sit in the Lady chapel
stained glass windows
their faces reflect
the entire spectrum of
light
their wimples float out
behind them
like horns or wings
all the souls of the earth
are their children
they claim

there is a motherhood they say
more expansive than
the generation of blood
there is a feeding of the
whole race
that can only be performed
in perfect silence
like the space between the water
and the fall of the water
like the absolute emptiness of a sky
broken by one perfect branch

(sometimes I think
a woman by herself
is like a breath
that can rise up and infuse
all of creation.)

Grande Jetée

some rhythms must remain unbroken

like a dancer in an
arabesque
some women cannot carry
a child
in their arms

some come to salvation
drawn by the hands of small children

some can only make their leaps

alone.

The Torrid Zone

you gave me
a piece of your
boyhood
Salina with its
summer corn
tender as breast buds
a library with
brown blinds
shut against
the heat
your father
speaking in tongues
against a hard blue sky
your first wife
playing the violin
as you listened
at the door

you sang me love songs
in Portuguese
and your mouth
was like the Amazon
full of beautiful fish
deep, slow, and dangerous.

The Kama Sutra of Kindness:
Position No. 1

in ancient Japan
after the first night
poems were exchanged
between the lovers

a branch of white blossoms
rests against the sky
you sleep
on my blue silk sheets

this brush brings words
to the blank rice paper
you touch me
and I speak

the third time
you enter a woman
it is mandatory
to say something kind

when I smell your hair
I think of wind and anemone

the imagination has
its own erogenous zones

your body bears me
to another season
thank you for resting
here with me
balanced on the crested moon.

The Kama Sutra of Kindness:
Position No. 2

should I greet you
as if
we had merely eaten
together one night
when the white birches
dripped wet
and lightning etched
black trees on your walls?

it is not love
I am asking

love comes from years
of breathing
skin to skin
tangled in each other's dreams
until each night
weaves another thread
in the same web
of blood and sleep

    and I have only
    passed through you quickly
    like light

and you have only
surrounded me suddenly
like flame

the lake is cold
the snows are sudden
the wild cherry bends
and winter's a burden

in your hand I feel
spring burn in the bud.

On Seeing Her Lover's Beard
As a Nest of Birds

when I am alone
I can still feel you
hovering over me
like a great
invisible bird

the heat from my hands
sends you higher and higher
drifting up on the thermals
to unbearable altitudes
my breath and bones support you
my skin is the sky of your descent

at night I dream
we lie on our backs
on a wing-shaped beach
of blue translucent sand
next to a nameless ocean
watching the hunt
of the black golondrinas.

On Time

we shall have time
in time
time to lie
in each other's arms
time slow as molasses
thick as maple syrup
hours of sweetness
whole days that rise and swell
like sap

we shall have years
of quietness
of blind night turnings
back to breast to arm
breath to breath
time to read of the decay
of entire empires
time to meditate on the implosion of stars
time to contemplate
small things at our leisure
the progress of a spider
across its web
the unfolding of a peony
the secret thoughts of ants

143

we will turn slow motion
into a new art form
philosophize on the gradual
eulogize snails and sloths
we will spend ten years
simply examining each other's fingernails
twenty years on the palms of our hands
an entire century devoted exclusively to
the warm curves of our ears

our lives will stretch out forever
like roads that lead across vast blooming deserts
there will be no impatience
no watches
no pain
and at the end
nothing to fear
not even the bright rush of death.

Walking the Sea to China

ten thousand miles
of blue desert
over the dolphin trail
over the whale road
out beyond the mouthtip of the land

the water springs beneath my feet
like gelatin
deep below I see
lovers wrapped
in each other's arms
among the circling angel fish

she has taken him
into her seaweed cove
under the cover of her current
to a bed of sand
where the octopus sing
of endless seductions
she has pillowed him down
among the soft sponges
placed gold coins from Spain
on his lips and eyes

whispered him stories
of doubloons and death
while I walk above
heading for Hilo
and its green crystal beach
papayas in season
and freshwater rain

at night I lie wrapped
in a manta ray cloak
rocking beneath
an ocean of stars
changing my constellations
each hour
like fresh sheets

I do things thought impossible
I touch the dragon mouth of Japan
I catch the rising sun
in my teeth each morning
like a hot biscuit

I continue for three hundred
days
step by step
I do not remember
that this cannot be
done

I do not remember
that the flesh
from long habit
pulls toward the core
drags to the center
flounders and falls

I shall not drown
nor die by water
I have broken free
from the passion of sinking
I am a part now
of all things
that float and fly

here
touch my fine scales
the balance I keep
my red feathered heart
my strange feet
that have left the land
to tread down the deep.

About the Author

Mary Mackey was born and raised in Indianapolis, Indiana and is related on her father's side to Mark Twain.

She has previously published three volumes of poetry: *Split Ends*, *One Night Stand*, and *Skin Deep*. She has also published a novella, *Immersion*, and three novels: *McCarthy's List*, *The Last Warrior Queen*, and her most recent work, *A Grand Passion*, which was inspired by a summer spent in Leningrad, where she had the chance to see performances by the Kirov Ballet.

Mary Mackey is a screenwriter as well as a novelist and poet. Her original screenplay *Silence*, directed by John Korty and starring the late Will Geer, won several awards. She also reviews regularly for *The San Francisco Chronicle* and has contributed to such widely diverse magazines as *The Saturday Evening Post*, *Ms. Magazine*, *The New American Review*, and *The Harvard Advocate*.

Mary Mackey has traveled widely and speaks French, Spanish, and Russian. She holds a Ph.D. in Comparative Literature and is currently a professor of English and Writer in Residence at California State University, Sacramento, where she teaches creative writing and film.

149

This book was typeset in 12-point Aldus,
a typeface designed for Stempel by
Hermann Zapf, based on the designs of
the Italian master, Aldus Manutius